UKULELE

THE CHARLIE BROWN COLLECTION™

INCLUDES TAB

ISBN 978-1-4950-5676-5

HAL•LEONARD® CORPORATION
7777 W. BLUEMOUND RD. P.O. BOX 13819 MILWAUKEE, WI 53213

PEANUTS © United Feature Syndicate, Inc.
www.snoopy.com

In Australia Contact:
Hal Leonard Australia Pty. Ltd.
4 Lentara Court
Cheltenham, Victoria, 3192 Australia
Email: ausadmin@halleonard.com.au

Visit Hal Leonard Online at
www.halleonard.com

CONTENTS

Blue Charlie Brown

By Vince Guaraldi

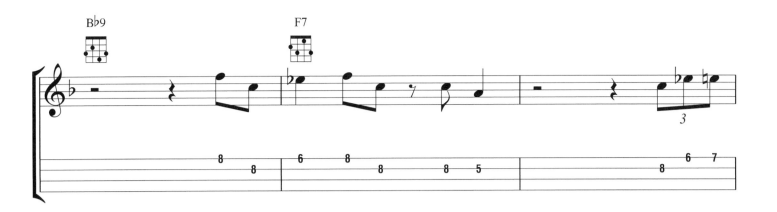

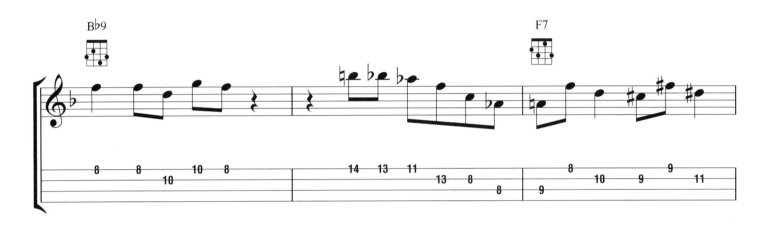

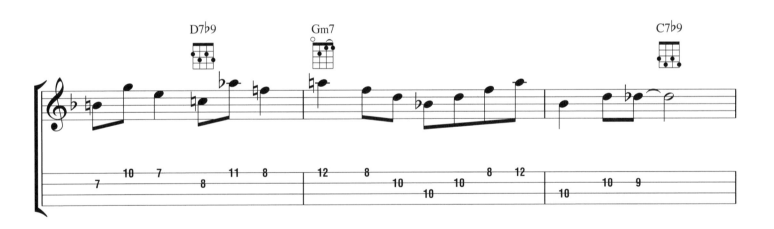

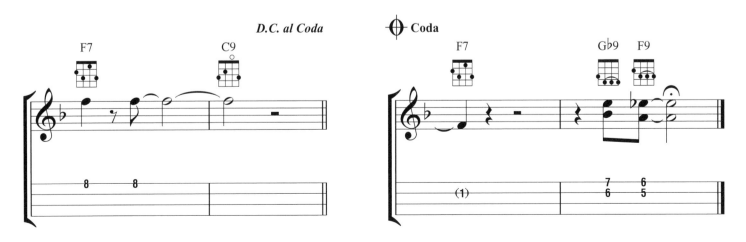

Charlie Brown Theme

By Vince Guaraldi

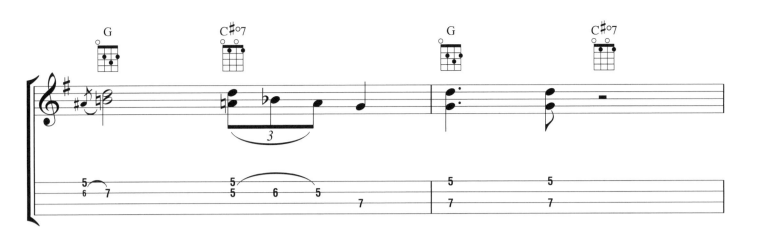

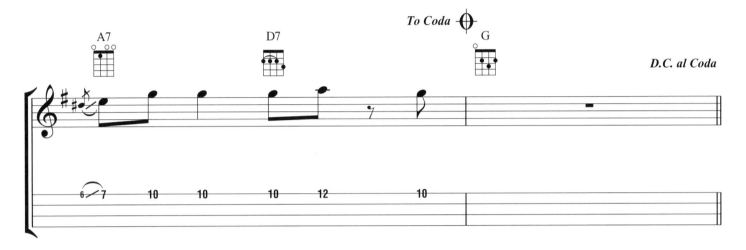

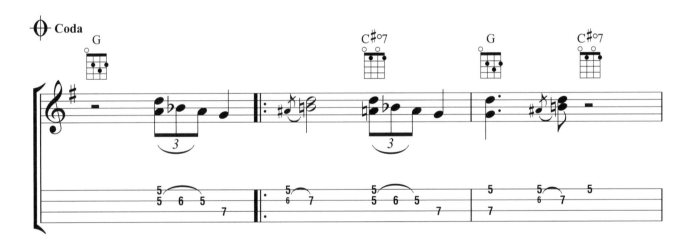

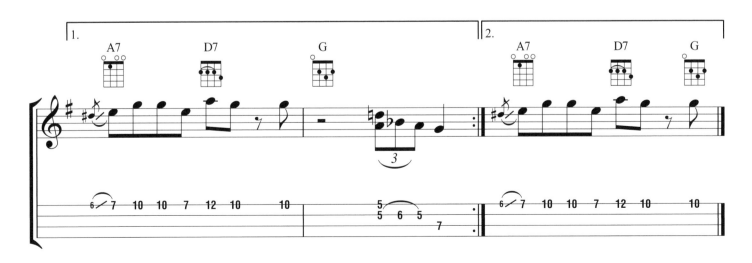

Christmas Is Coming

from A CHARLIE BROWN CHRISTMAS

By Vince Guaraldi

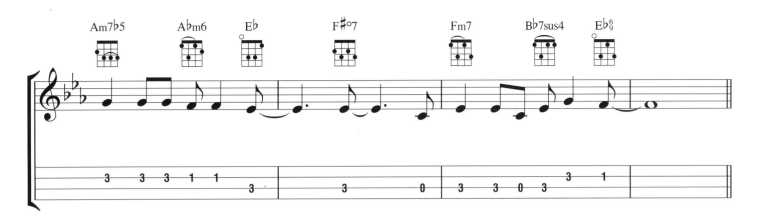

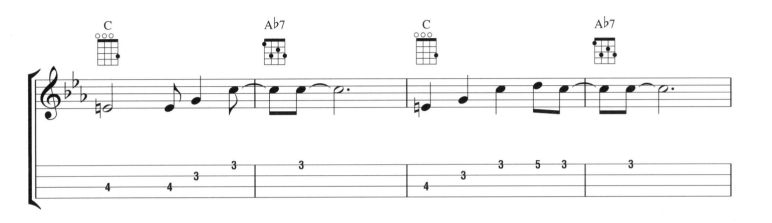

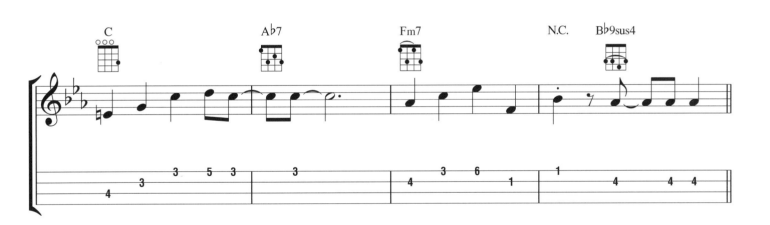

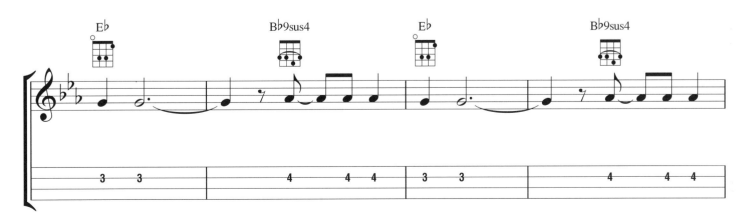

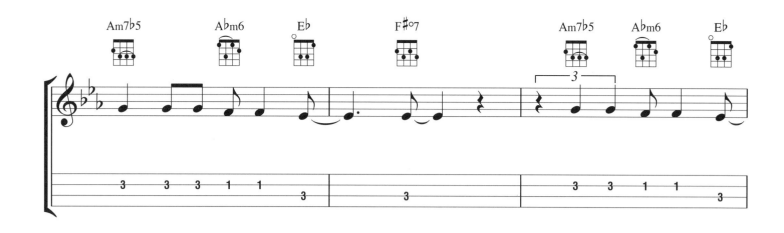

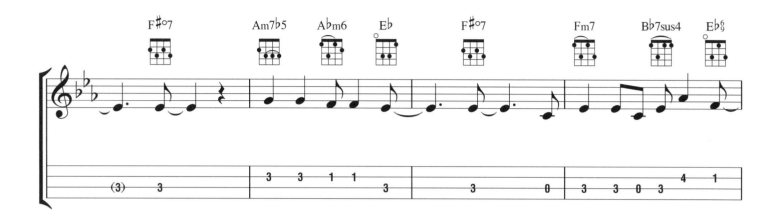

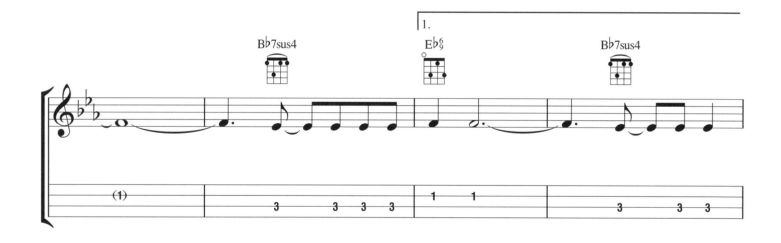

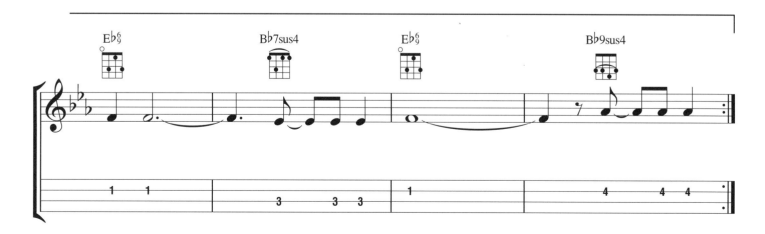

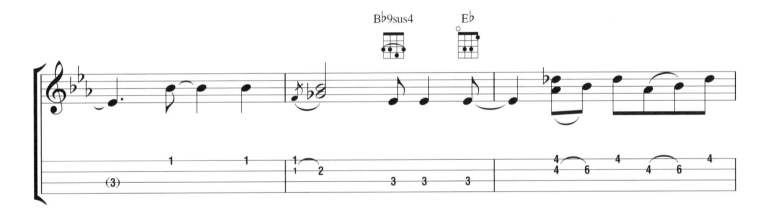

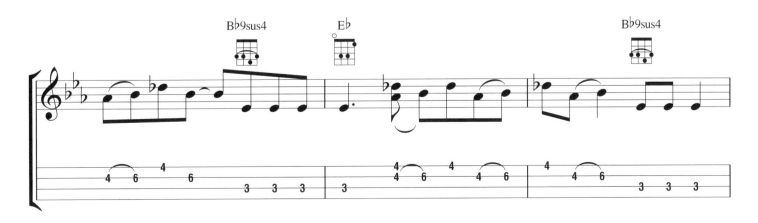

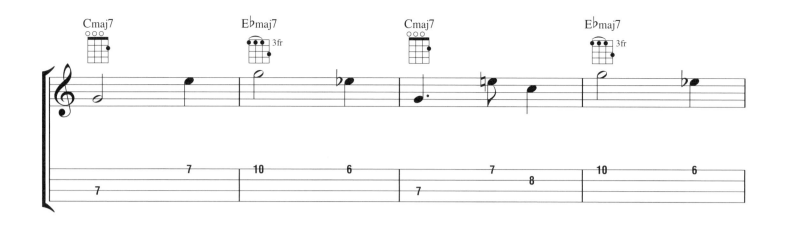

To Coda ⊕

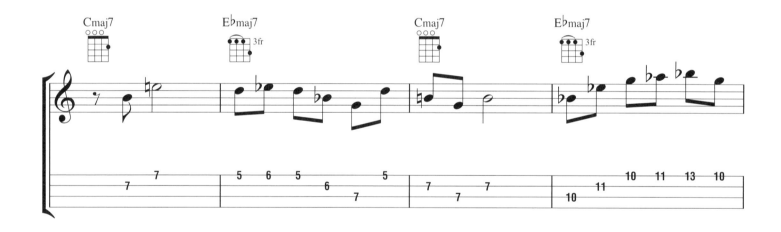

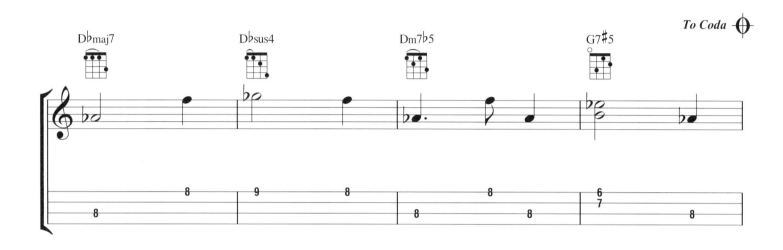

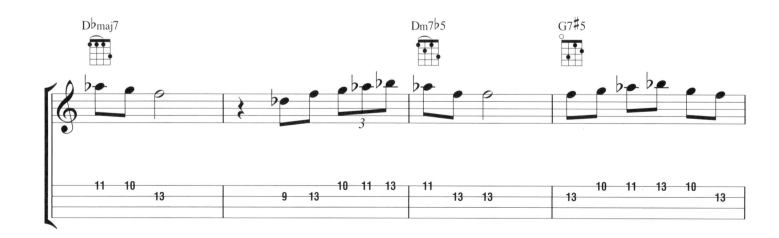

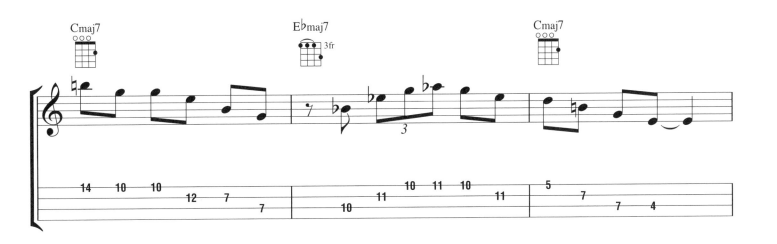

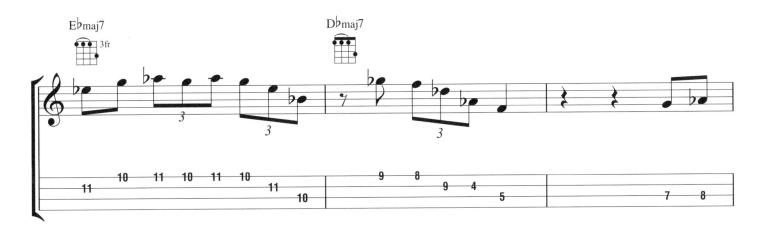

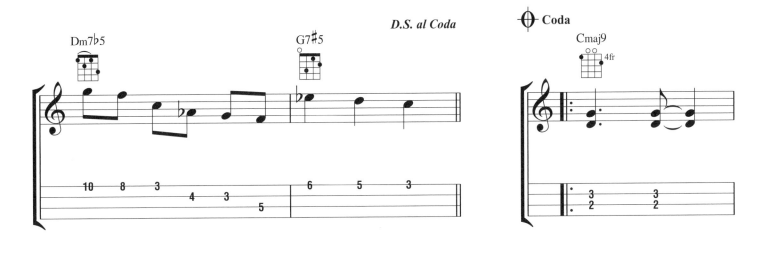

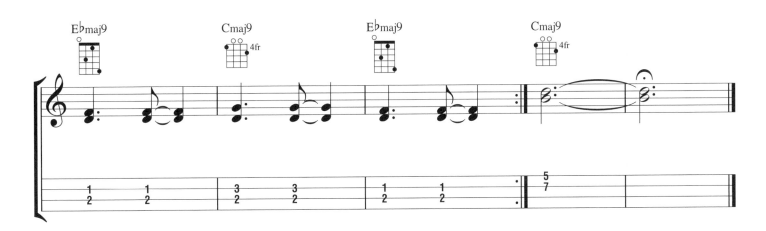

Christmas Time Is Here

from A CHARLIE BROWN CHRISTMAS

Words by Lee Mendelson
Music by Vince Guaraldi

Slowly, unhurried

Christ - mas time is here, hap - pi - ness and cheer.

Fun for all that chil - dren call their fa - v'rite time of year.

Snow - flakes in the air, car - ols ev - 'ry - where.

Old - en times and an - cient rhymes of love and dreams to share.

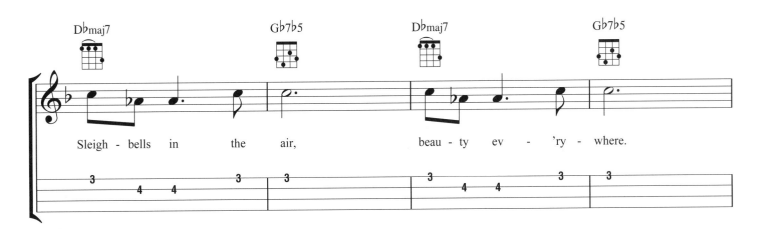

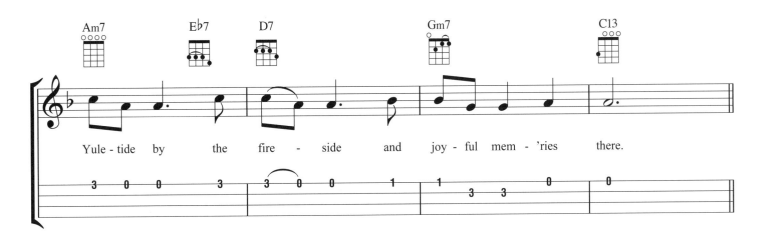

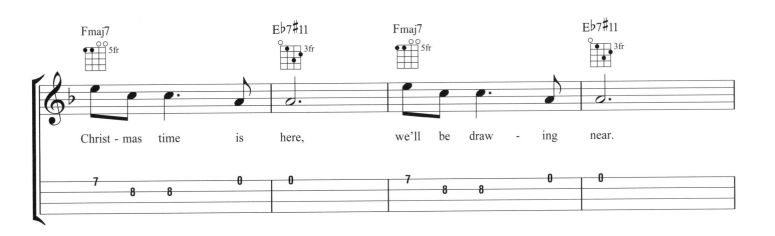

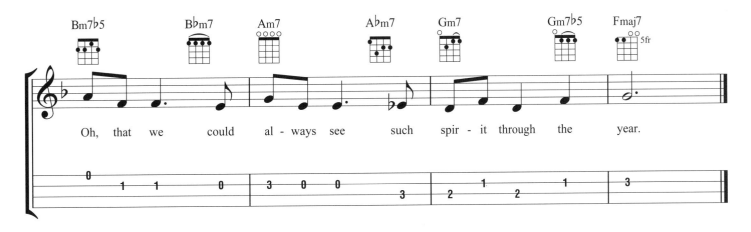

The Great Pumpkin Waltz

By Vince Guaraldi

Moderately fast, leisurely

Happiness Theme

By Vince Guaraldi

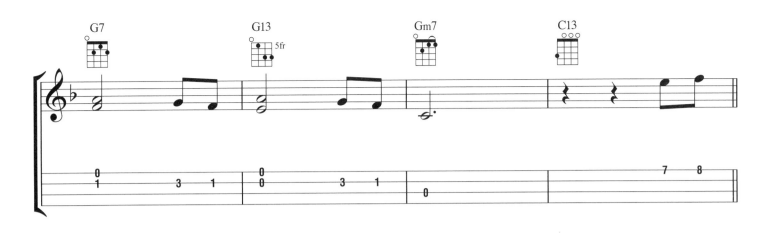

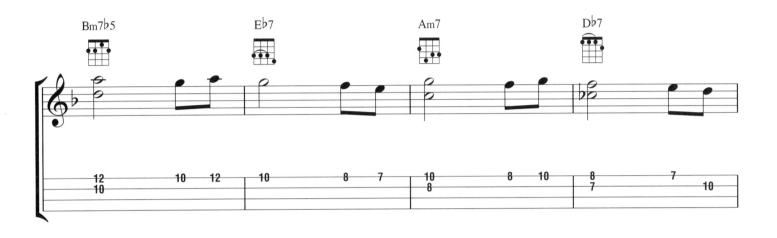

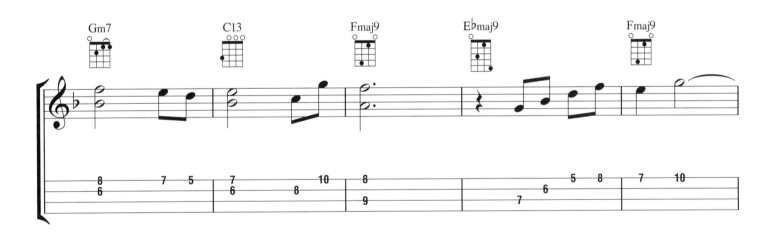

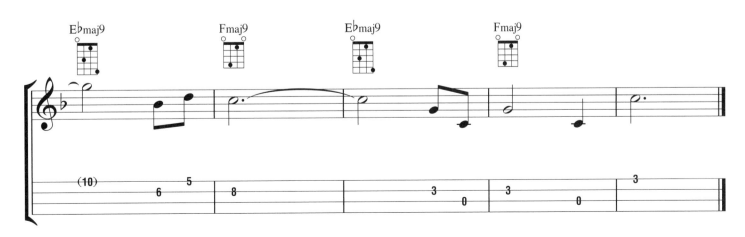

He's Your Dog, Charlie Brown

By Vince Guaraldi

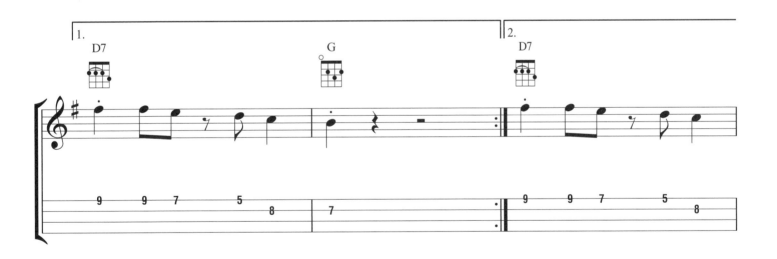

Joe Cool

By Vince Guaraldi

Linus and Lucy

By Vince Guaraldi

Love Will Come

By Vince Guaraldi

Peppermint Patty

By Vince Guaraldi

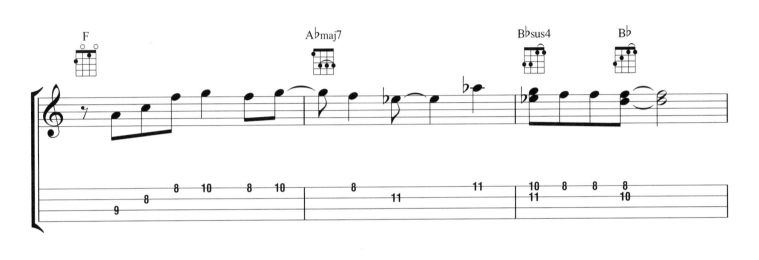

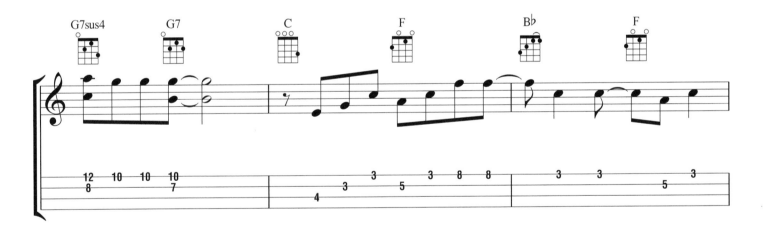

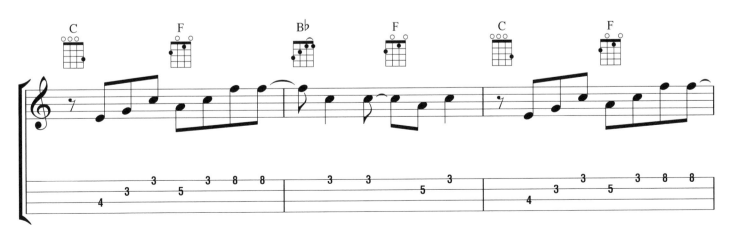

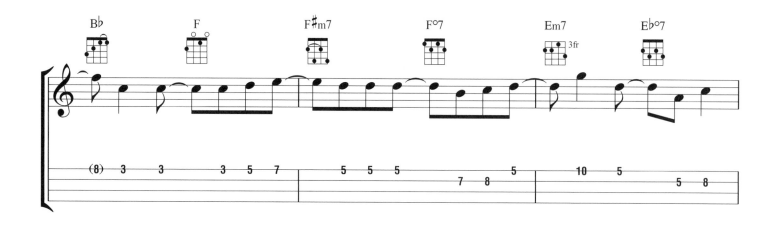

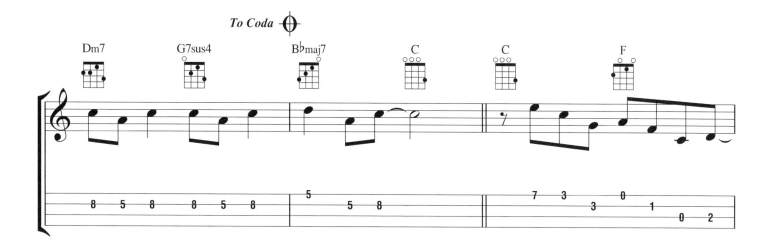

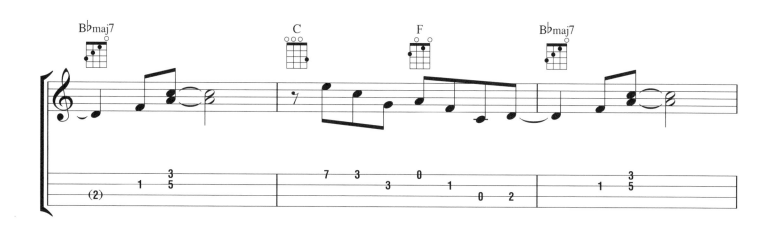

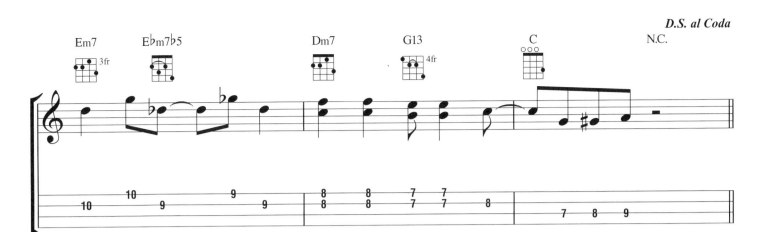

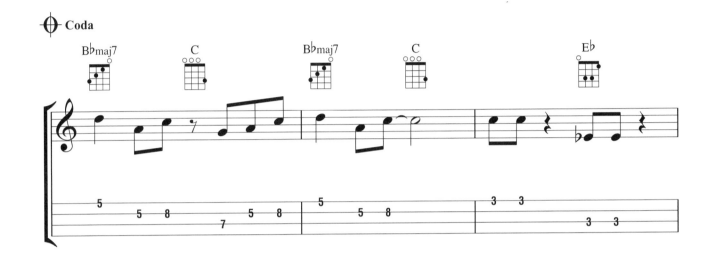

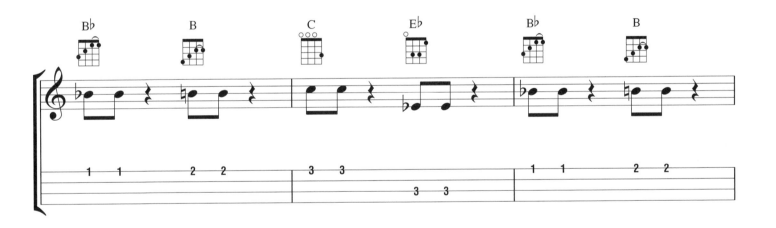

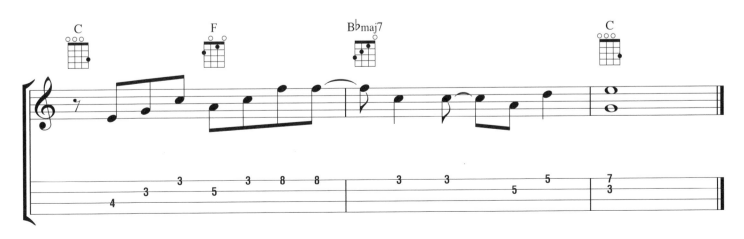

Schroeder

By Vince Guaraldi

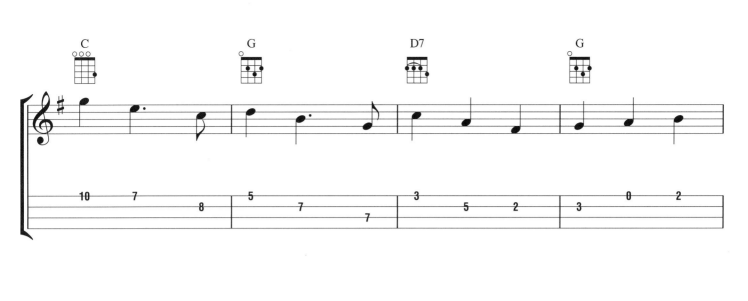

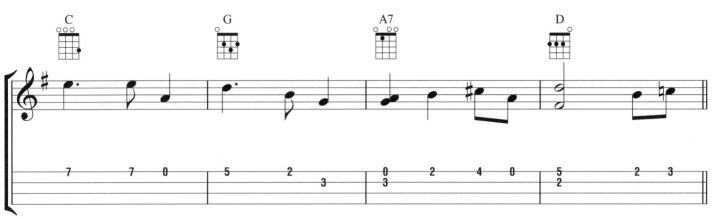

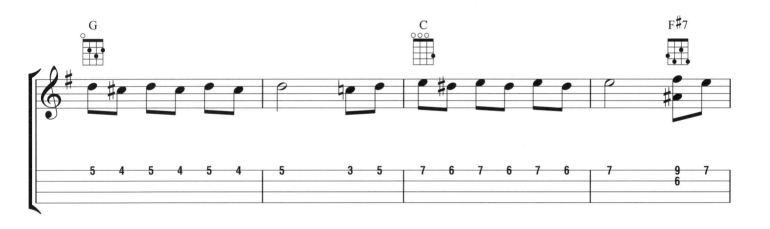

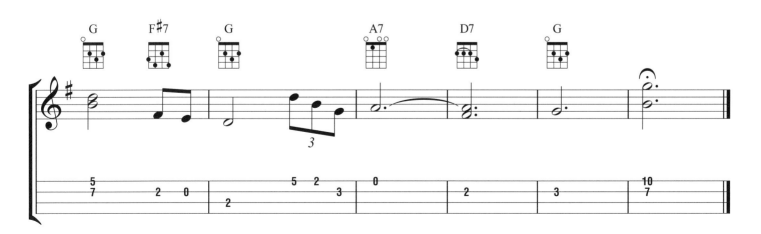

Skating

By Vince Guaraldi

39

Surfin' Snoopy

By Vince Guaraldi

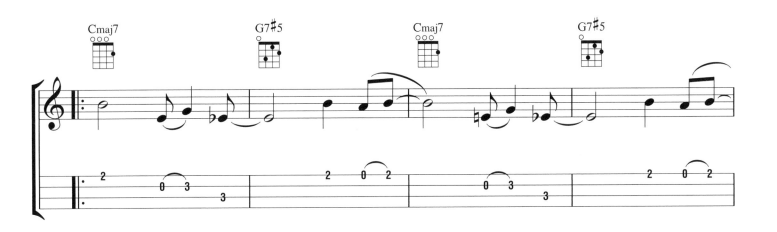

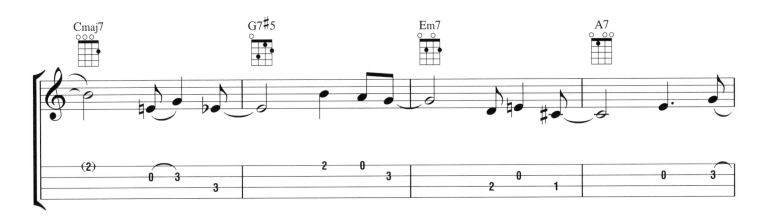

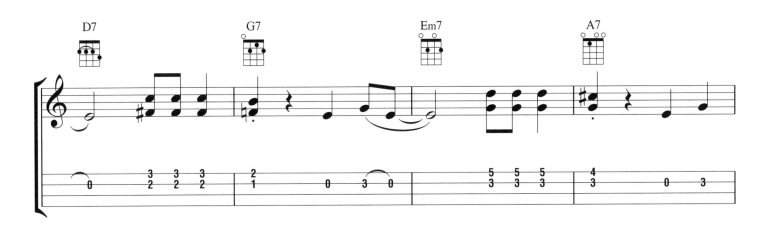

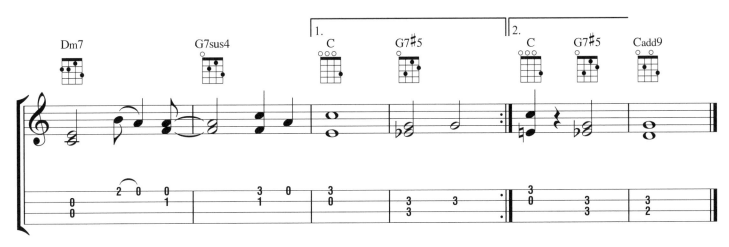

You're in Love, Charlie Brown

By Vince Guaraldi

Red Baron

By Vince Guaraldi

Moderately, in 2

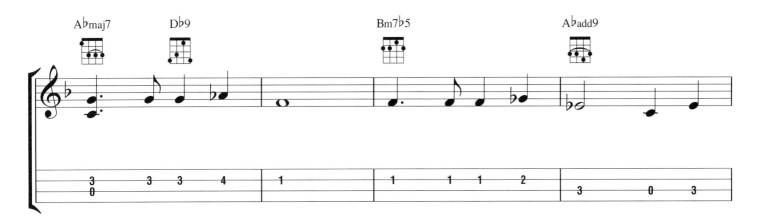

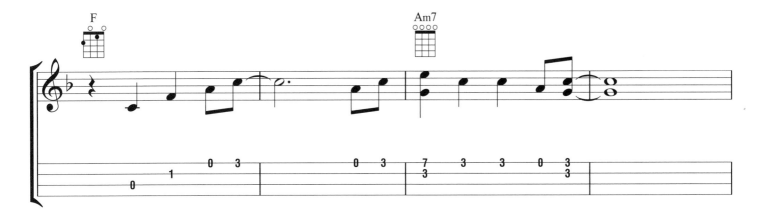

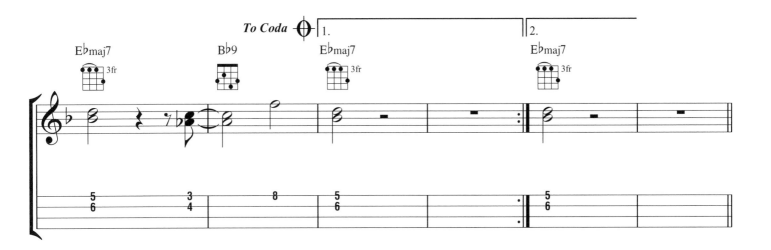

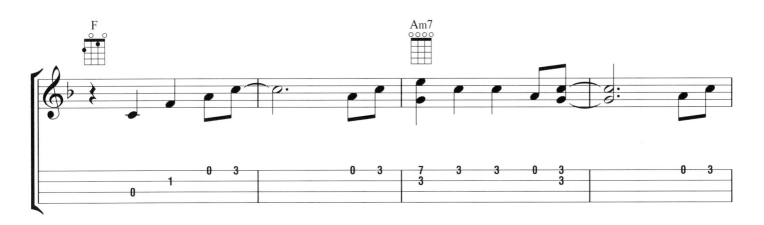

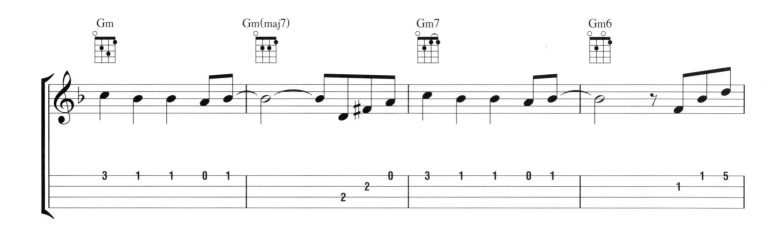

D.S. al Coda

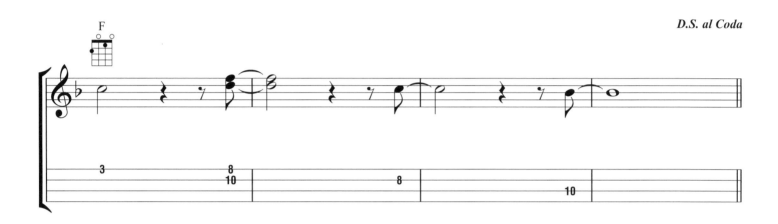

Coda

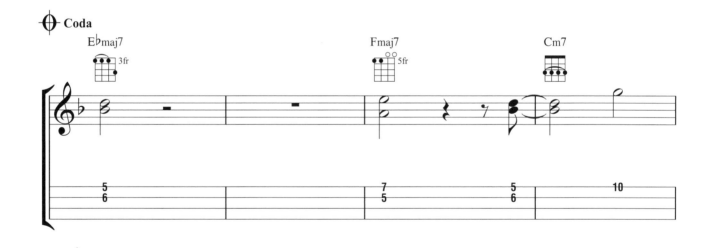

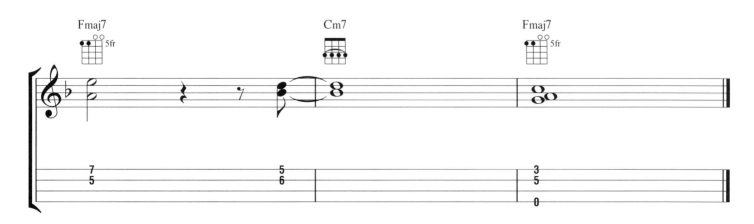